WOMEN WHO WON'T BE SILENCED
THE STORIES OF STRONG WOMEN

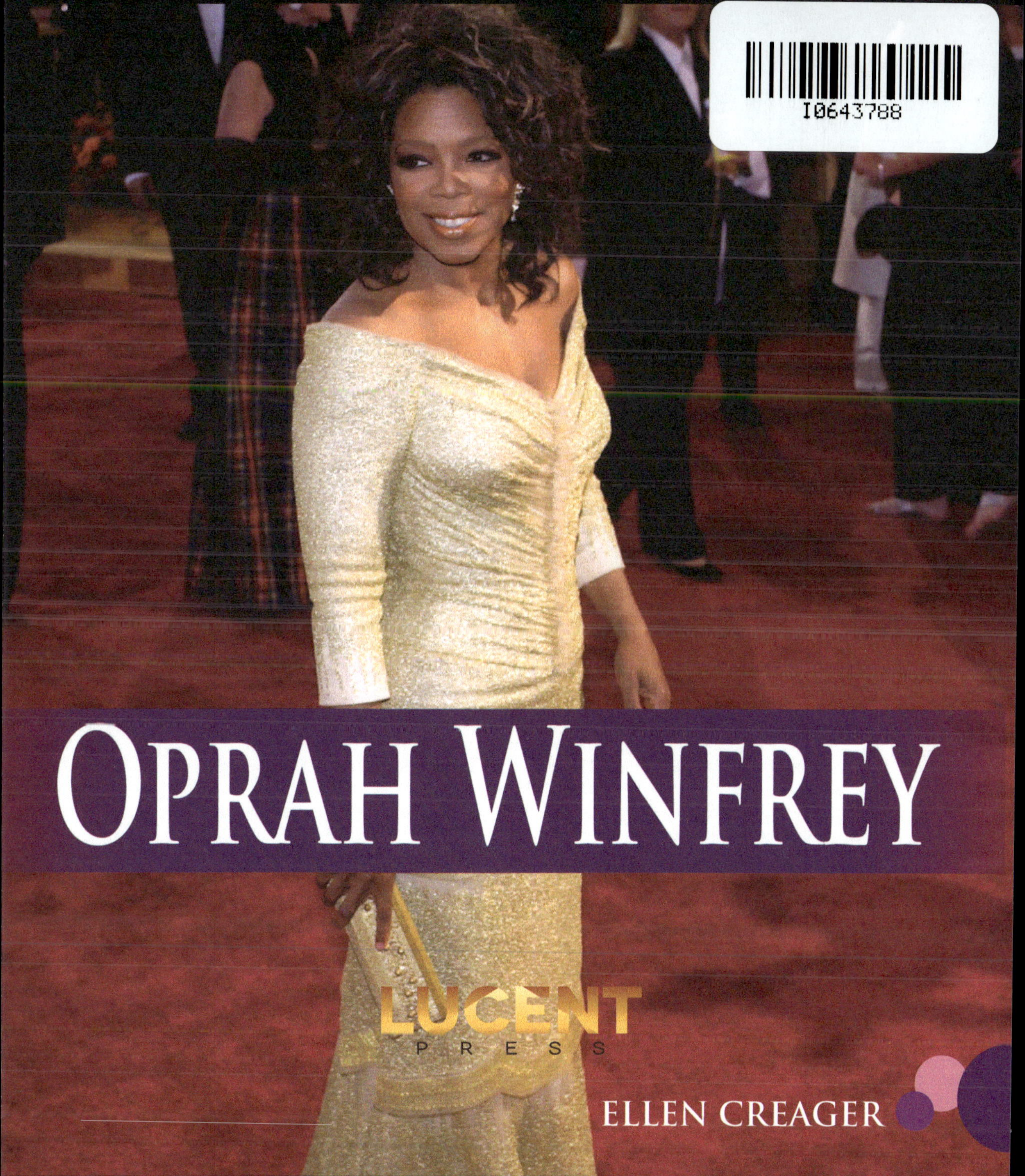

OPRAH WINFREY

LUCENT PRESS

ELLEN CREAGER

Published in 2019 by
Lucent Press, an Imprint of Greenhaven Publishing, LLC
353 3rd Avenue
Suite 255
New York, NY 10010

Developed and produced for Rosen by BlueApple*Works* Inc.

Managing Editor for BlueApple*Works*: Melissa McClellan
Designer: Tibor Choleva
Photo Research: Jane Reid
Editor: Marcia Abramson

Photo Credits: cover, title page, p. 19, 44, 56 Featureflash Photo Agency/Shutterstock.com; background Vladitto/Shutterstock; p. 4, 30, 32, 35, 42 Kathy Hutchins/Shutterstock.com; p. 7, 25 bottom Tinseltown/Shutterstock.com; p. 8 John Barrett/Keystone Press; p. 11 Andrew Jameson/Creative Commons; p. 12 Marylandstater /Public Domain; p. 13 Antandrus /Creative Commons; p. 14, 23, 26, 40 Everett Collection/Shutterstock.com; p. 17 Warner Bros. Pictures/Photofest; p. 21, 38 Globe Photos/Keystone Press; p. 24 CBS/Photofest; p. 25 top DFree/Shutterstock.com; p. 28 TY Lim/Shutterstock.com; p. 29 Ken Wolter/Shutterstock.com; p. 33 Stokkete /Shutterstock; p. 34 Joe Seer/Shutterstock.com; p. 37 Edward A Ornelas/Keystone Press; p. 41 Sundry Photography/Shutterstock.com; p. 46 FAME Pictures/KEYSTONE Press; p. 48 Rena Schild/Shutterstock.com; p. 51 PMK/KEYSTONE Press; p. 52 Walt Disney Studios Motion Pictures/Photofest; p. 55 ZUMA Press, Inc./Alamy Stock Photo

Cataloging-in-Publication-Data
Names: Creager, Ellen.
Title: Oprah Winfrey / Ellen Creager.
Description: New York : Lucent Press, 2019. | Series: Women who won't be silenced: the stories of strong women | Includes glossary and index.
Identifiers: ISBN 9781534566415 (pbk.) | ISBN 9781534566422 (library bound) | ISBN 9781534566439 (ebook)
Subjects: LCSH: Winfrey, Oprah--Juvenile literature. | Television personalities--Biography--Juvenile literature. | African American television personalities--Biography--Juvenile literature. | Actors--United States--Biography--Juvenile literature. | African American actors--Biography--Juvenile literature.
Classification: LCC PN1992.4.W56 C743 2019 | DDC 791.4502'8092 B--dc23

Manufactured in the United States of America

CPSIA Compliance Information: Batch #BW19KL: For Further Information contact: Greenhaven Publishing LLC, New York, New York at 1-844-317-7404.

CONTENTS

CHAPTER 1

WHO IS OPRAH WINFREY?

So famous that she is recognized by just one name, Oprah is both a brand and a powerful woman.

For 25 years she was the popular host of a television talk show seen by millions. The show tackled every subject, whether scandalous or noble, including her constant struggles with her weight.

Her charm and **empathy** made viewers see her as a friend, not just a TV host.

Since 2011, when her show ended, her impact has only expanded. She is a billionaire **philanthropist** generously giving away millions to charities. She started *O, The Oprah Magazine* and a cable TV network. She writes books and stars in films. Today she is equal parts business tycoon, actress, and role model for many across the nation. Her goal, she says, is to help all people live their best lives.

Part of Oprah Winfrey's childhood was spent in poverty and instability. Yet even as a young girl, her warm, velvety voice and public speaking skills made her stand out. All her life, whether speaking in church, as a broadcaster, or acting in films, her voice and magnetic personality got her noticed. In 2018, she gave a memorable speech about the power of women and girls so stirring that admirers even urged her to run for president of the United States.

Today, Oprah is one of the richest and most influential people in the United States. Yet as she grows older, she increasingly has harnessed her stardom for good in the world.

With a life full of improbable events that took her from poor, rural Mississippi to the glamorous life of a cultural **icon**, "one can't help but be amazed at how far Oprah has come," wrote scholar Henry Louis Gates Jr. "She is almost like a character in a fairy tale."

"I BELIEVE IN MY OWN POSSIBILITIES, SO I CAN DO WHATEVER I FEEL CAPABLE OF DOING, AND I FEEL I CAN DO IT ALL."

– Oprah Winfrey interview with TV Guide*'s R. C. Smith, 1986*

By 1993, when this photo was taken, Oprah was a great success. According to a family story, she started early – interviewing her corncob doll and birds on the fence when she was only three!

CHAPTER 2

EARLY YEARS

Oprah Winfrey came into the world as a bright light on a dim stage. Her given name was "Orpah," after a character in the Book of Ruth in the Bible. But in usage, the odd baby name quickly morphed into "Oprah," and it stuck. Her middle name is Gail.

She was born January 29, 1954, in rural Kosciusko, Mississippi. Her teenage mother, Vernita Lee, soon moved to Milwaukee, Wisconsin, leaving her own mother in charge of raising Oprah. A strict lady who believed in whipping with a switch, Hattie Mae Lee also taught Oprah to read and write by age 5. She was promoted to first grade on her first day of kindergarten. Young Oprah also had a fine speaking voice. She memorized many poems and Bible passages and recited them at church and clubs, astonishing the members, who called her "Little Speaker."

Then, bad luck came calling. At age 6, Oprah went to Milwaukee to live with her mother and half-sister, Patricia Lee, in a run-down rooming house. A year later, Oprah briefly went to live with her father, Vernon Winfrey, in Nashville, Tennessee, only to be taken back by her mother.

Those were rough years. Oprah was very smart, but soon her life bent into a troubled shape. Her intelligence meant she was selected to be bused to a suburban high school for ninth grade, but it didn't work out. By age 13 and 14 she was rebelling and running away. Oprah was also the victim of abuse before her strict father and his wife, Zelma, agreed to take Oprah to live with them permanently in Nashville. This would prove a life-saver for the young teen.

Soon after she arrived to live with him, her father found out Oprah was pregnant. Oprah's baby was born too early and died within a month. Her father, who owns a barbershop, told her sternly that from then on she needed to make something of her life, study hard, and not disappoint him. It was a turning point.

"WHEN I MOVE THROUGH THE WORLD I BRING ALL MY HISTORY WITH ME. ALL THE PEOPLE WHO PAVED THE WAY FOR ME ARE THE BEST PART OF WHO I AM."

– *Oprah Winfrey's book* What I Know for Sure, *page 48*

Oprah was voted Most Popular in her graduating class at East Nashville High, now a school for grades 5-12.

Oprah blossomed at East Nashville High School. She was a straight-A student and student council president. She gave a speech at the local Elks Club that won her a college scholarship. When she was 17, a man at local radio station, WVOL, heard her beautiful speaking voice and asked her to read the news on the air, part-time. That led to other opportunities. She even was crowned Miss Fire Prevention in Nashville.

Her father was proud when she began college at Tennessee State University, majoring in speech and drama. While in college, she became Miss Black Tennessee. The talented Oprah also was hired by WTVF-TV in Nashville as a news reader in 1973 when she was just 19 years old.

"Baltimore grew me up," Oprah says of her years at WJZ. She faced some discrimination and harassment, but also learned a lot and made lifelong friends.

Then, in 1976, she was offered her big break. A major TV station in Baltimore, Maryland, WJZ, wanted her to become a news anchor. Leaving behind a serious boyfriend, her family, and her college days (a few credits short of graduating), Oprah Winfrey, 22, headed north to the big city. What a jolt it was.

In Baltimore, it turned out that she was a **mediocre** news anchor. She got too involved with her subjects. She did not like the sad topics. After a year, her disappointed bosses transferred her to become co-host of *People Are Talking*, a morning talk show.

Eureka! She was a smash success. Soon, Baltimore was buzzing about Oprah Winfrey. Her show broke ratings records, and she was on her way to becoming a star.

After a few years other TV stations came calling – including one that would change her life, WLS-TV in Chicago.

CHANGE OF FORTUNES

Young Oprah dreamed of having a beautiful home. Now she has lots of them. Not bad for a girl so poor, kids teased her for having clothes made from potato sacks. Her main home is a mansion called The Promised Land on 65 acres near the ocean in Montecito, California. It is worth about $95 million. She also has a home and farm in Hawaii, plus properties in Colorado, Florida, New Jersey, Nashville, and Chicago. She travels between them on her private jet worth $42 million.

Oprah fell in love with her California mansion when she went there for a party in 1991. It was not on the market, but she convinced the owners to sell! She says she named it The Promised Land because Dr. Martin Luther King Jr. "said he would not get to the promised land but one day we might ... I think it's a fulfillment of the promise that Dr. King spoke of."

One of Oprah's favorite guests, singer Mariah Carey, joined her for a live telecast from New York City in September 2009. Mariah was on the show 22 times!

CHAPTER 3

THE OPRAH WINFREY SHOW

During the 25 years that Oprah Winfrey had her national TV talk show (1986-2011), she did an astonishing 4,561 episodes and interviewed more than 30,000 guests.

That chapter of her life began when WLS-TV in Chicago hired her to host its struggling *AM Chicago* show. At just 29, she suddenly was making $200,000 a year. The ratings boomed immediately, as the bold, bright TV host charmed Chicago viewers. She was so popular that the name of the show was changed to *The Oprah Winfrey Show*. It then was **syndicated** to other TV stations across the nation, which got her even more viewers.

Over the next two decades she would interview everyone from the singer Michael Jackson to First Lady Michelle Obama, and from fashion experts to couples in marriages gone wrong.

"I ALWAYS KNEW I WAS BORN FOR GREATNESS."

– Oprah Winfrey interview with New York Times Magazine *writer Barbara Grizzuti, June 11, 1989*

Many topics she covered sound common now, but she was among the first to put many controversial and personal subjects on the air. The secret of her success as a TV host boiled down to two things: she had a knack for asking the questions that everybody wanted to know the answers to, and she shared a lot of herself with the audience.

On the show, for example, Oprah many times talked about her struggles with weight and dieting. One time, after she lost 67 pounds, she wheeled a red wagon onto the stage with a giant rubber blob representing the fat she had lost. She once shared with the audience that she had been sexually abused as a child — a bombshell that made other women share their stories.

Oprah Winfrey also had another ingredient that led to her success on the show: nobody worked harder than she did. She was in charge. She was driven to be a star and a success, and she was willing to put in the work needed to make it happen.

"ANYTHING CAN BE A MIRACLE, A BLESSING, AN OPPORTUNITY IF YOU CHOOSE TO SEE IT THAT WAY."

– Oprah Winfrey's book What I Know for Sure, *page 46*

OPRAH IN THE MOVIES

Oprah was cast as Sofia in the 1985 film *The Color Purple* because of a fluke. Movie producer Quincy Jones happened to be in Chicago when he turned on the TV to *The Oprah Winfrey Show* in his hotel room. He immediately decided to cast Oprah for the role. She later was nominated for an Academy Award for best supporting actress.

A film Oprah both produced and starred in was *Beloved* in 1998. The $53-million, three-hour film based on Toni Morrison's searing novel of an escaped slave got good reviews but did very poorly at the box office. It was one of the few projects that even Oprah's magic touch could not save.

Undeterred, Oprah went on to star in many film and television roles.

Oprah played a strong woman in a troubled marriage with Harpo (Willard E. Pugh) in *The Color Purple*.

FAME AND FORTUNE

In 1986, Winfrey formed Harpo Productions, Inc. — a name chosen because Harpo is Oprah spelled backwards. She obtained the rights to produce her own show. She built a big studio in Chicago.

The money began rolling in. She bought an $800,000 condo on the Chicago shoreline that had gold faucets in the bathrooms. She rode in a chauffeured limousine. She also bought a big farm in Indiana. In 1988, she suddenly was making $30 million a year. By 1990, the show was seen by 20 million viewers around the world, and she was worth $250 million. By 1993, she was on the cover of *Forbes* magazine as the richest entertainer in America. She became good friends with other famous people such as the poet Maya Angelou.

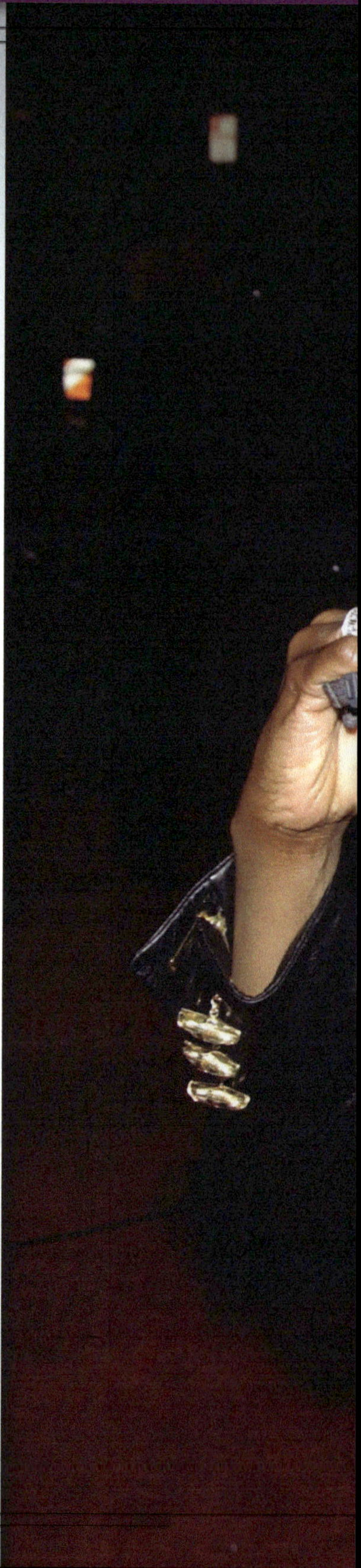

Oprah was the People's Choice for Best Talk Show Host in 2004 (above) and 1988.

Yet, not everyone liked Oprah. Some critics said her shows were in bad taste and showcased human misery, focusing on racy, trashy content to get higher ratings. Some black critics said she was too focused on being a crowd-pleaser, avoiding topics about racial injustice.

Other similar shows popped up that were even more **lurid**. One day in 1988, fighting for ratings, Oprah Winfrey hosted some **skinheads**. They were so hateful that she made them leave in the middle of the show. The next year she was interviewing a man, his wife, and his mistress. She realized in the middle of the show how humiliating it was for the wife and vowed never to do a show again that would hurt someone.

"NEVER AGAIN WILL I PUT MYSELF IN A POSITION TO USE MY STAGE, MY PLATFORM OR MYSELF TO PUBLICLY EMBARRASS OR HURT ANYONE."

– Oprah Winfrey recounting her decision in 1989 to change her show's focus, in an essay written by her on the website Leanin.org

Oprah says her personal trainer, Bob Greene (right), helped her realize that her life and her show needed a new direction.

ROAD TO WELLNESS

In the 1990s, Oprah changed her show's focus to wellness for women. She did shows on spiritual improvement, getting healthy, improving your finances, and helping others. She had frequent guests whom she later helped get their own TV shows, such as Dr. Phil McGraw, Rachael Ray, Iyanla Vanzant, Suze Orman, and Dr. Mehmet Oz.

During the years of *The Oprah Winfrey Show*, Oprah grew and changed before the eyes of the audience. The show was seen in 149 countries. She became so famous and powerful, so much a part of the culture, that when ordinary people had something unusual happen, their friends would say, "You should go on Oprah."

Still, as her success grew, so did expectations — especially from her family. They came out of the woodwork to ask for support. She bought houses and cars for her father and stepmother and gave money to her estranged mother, half-sister Patricia Lee Lloyd, and half-brother Jeffrey Lee. She put her sister through drug rehab multiple times before Lloyd died in 2003 of an overdose (her brother died in 1989 of AIDS). She also put her nieces through school. One huge surprise happened in 2010 when she found out she had another half-sister, also named Patricia. That sister was welcomed by Oprah and she did not ask for money. She only wanted to be acknowledged as family. Oprah ended up buying her a house and sending her to college.

In 2011, Oprah announced it was time to end her show after 25 years. She was ready for the next act.

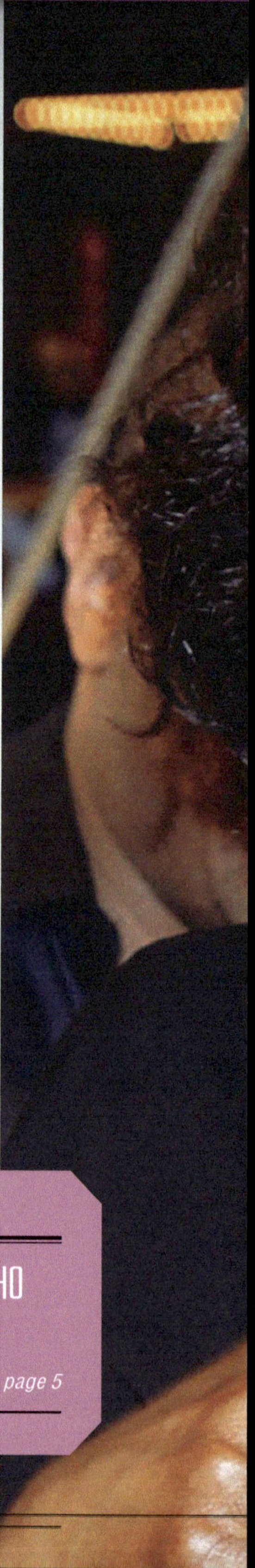

"FOR AS LONG AS I CAN REMEMBER I'VE BEEN THE KIND OF PERSON WHO WANTS TO SHARE THE THINGS THAT MAKE LIFE BETTER."

– Oprah Winfrey's book Food, Health, and Happiness, *page 5*

OPRAH'S BIGGEST GIVEAWAY

In the final years of *The Oprah Winfrey Show* she began a feature called "Oprah's Favorite Things." Once a year she would announce to the studio audience a list of her favorite products, and the audience would get many of the freebies — everything from washing machines to cashmere sweaters, lip balm, and cruises. Her biggest-ever giveaway happened September 13, 2004. She gave away free Pontiac G6 cars worth $29,000 each to all 276 members of the studio audience. General Motors paid for the cars as a promotion.

"It was the most fun I'd ever had on TV," she later wrote.

A CAREER BOOST FROM OPRAH

Many of Oprah's favorite guests have become superstars in their own right. Here are three of the biggest names who started their rise with Oprah:

Rachael Ray began appearing with Oprah in 2005. She soon became one of America's favorite lifestyle and cooking experts with her own TV shows and product lines ranging from cookware to dog food.

Nate Berkus started out as a guest decorator for Oprah's show in 2002. He's been on the fast track ever since. His home decor products, sold in stores and online, have made him a huge success. He's written books, including the huge best seller, *The Things That Matter*. He had his own TV show and began a new one with his husband, Jeremiah, in 2017.

Dr. Phil McGraw never thought he'd be a TV star. That all changed when he was working as a legal consultant in 1996 and helped Oprah with a case. She liked his direct approach to life and began featuring him as a life coach and relationship expert. Now he is a best-selling author with his own TV talk show, produced by Oprah's company.

The premiere of *The Great Debaters* was a gala event for Oprah in 2007. She was one of the producers of the film based on the inspiring story of the debate team at a historically black college in Texas in 1935.

CHAPTER 4

THE OPRAH BRAND

During the final years of *The Oprah Winfrey Show*, Oprah turned away from gritty problem shows and more toward self-help topics and uplifting themes. She also began new ventures that blossomed.

OPRAH'S BOOK CLUB

In 1996 Oprah decided she wanted Americans to do more reading and know more about authors. From 1996 to 2002, she chose six to eight new novels each season to feature on her show. Her promotion guaranteed the books would become instant best sellers.

Starting in 2002, she even began using her power to promote classic novels, which also jumped to the top of the best-seller lists.

The book club ended in 2010 with the last novel she recommended, Charles Dickens' *Great Expectations*.

"I WANT TO GET THE WHOLE COUNTRY READING AGAIN."

– Oprah Winfrey introducing her book club, 1996

Like the ones she writes, books about Oprah also fly out of bookstores. For example, her personal chef Rosie Daley cooked up a best seller called *In the Kitchen with Rosie: Oprah's Favorite Recipes.*

BOOKS BY OPRAH

Oprah has written or co-written many books. Another, tentatively titled *The Life You Want*, was first set to be published in January 2017, but in 2016 it was announced that it was being postponed.

Here are some of the books she has published:

Make the Connection: Ten Steps to a Better Body – and a Better Life (1996). A health/diet book co-written with her personal trainer, Bob Greene.

What I Know for Sure (2014). A book of her *O Magazine* columns.

The Wisdom of Sundays (2017). Spiritual advice drawn from interviews she did on her TV show, *Super Soul Sunday.*

Food, Health, and Happiness (2017). A recipe and personal health book.

WEIGHT WATCHERS CONNECTION

One powerful example of the Oprah brand in action is her connection to the weight-loss company Weight Watchers. In 2015, Oprah Winfrey bought a 10-percent stake in the company for $43 million. She also became the Weight Watchers spokesperson. As soon as that happened, company stock soared.

She may now weigh less, but her wallet weighs more. She reportedly lost 30 to 40 pounds using the Weight Watchers program, while the value of her investment grew to $445 million by 2018.

Oprah tried Weight Watchers first before becoming the company spokesperson. She liked the healthy approach and signed on after losing 15 pounds.

"I WILL HAVE A WONDERFUL LIFE."

– Oprah Winfrey interview with TV Guide*'s R. C. Smith, 1986*

5 THINGS THAT MIGHT SURPRISE YOU ABOUT OPRAH

1. She is left-handed.
2. She loves bathtubs and baths. She once had a bathtub made for herself in the shape of her body.
3. She has kept a daily journal on and off since she was 15.
4. She ran a marathon in 1994.
5. She is afraid of flying over the ocean, even though she has a house in Hawaii.

OPRAH'S BEST FRIEND

Some people knew Oprah long before she became a brand or household name. One of those people is Gayle King, her best friend. The two met when both worked in Baltimore at WJZ-TV in 1976.

Oprah credits her friend with keeping her going in her darkest times and being there in her happiest times, too. "In all my triumphs – in every good and great thing that has ever happened to me – Gayle has been my boldest cheerleader," Oprah wrote in her 2014 book, *What I Know for Sure.* For several years Gayle King hosted a talk show on Oprah's cable network, OWN. She currently is a co-host of *CBS This Morning* and the editor-at-large of *O Magazine.*

Gayle King began talking with Oprah while caught in a snowstorm – and they never stopped.

O Magazine has more readers than any other American women's magazine, according to its publishers.

O MAGAZINE

The glossy self-help publication named after Oprah launched in 2000 and was an immediate hit. It has a circulation of 2.4 million.

One reason for its continuing popularity is that Oprah's picture is on every single cover. Inside, many articles focus on "your best life," and Oprah's advice column, "What I Know for Sure," is featured.

"I BELIEVE PART OF MY CALLING ON EARTH IS TO HELP PEOPLE CONNECT TO IDEAS THAT EXPAND THEIR VISION OF WHO THEY REALLY ARE AND ALL THEY CAN BE."

– Oprah Winfrey's book What I Know for Sure, *page 10*

Oprah says she always believed "that one day I would create a television network ... my show was just the beginning of what the future could hold."

OWN NETWORK

After *The Oprah Winfrey Show* ended in 2011, Oprah immediately started her own TV cable network, OWN – the Oprah Winfrey Network. It carried her *Super Soul Sunday* interview program, plus original programming that focused on women, such as *Queen Sugar*.

She told an interviewer for *Vogue* in 2017 that she had hoped to use the network to run only inspirational, spiritual shows, but that idea flopped. "I learned you have got to give them … snackable spirituality," she said, "snackable, digestible moments in an entertaining format, so people can receive it."

In 2017, she sold a majority stake of OWN to Discovery Communications for $70 million but remained chief executive.

THE OPRAH BUMP

Marketers have a name for the golden touch that Oprah Winfrey has when associated with a product. It is called the "Oprah bump" or the "Oprah Effect." If she mentions a product, writer, or idea, everybody listens. The power of her **charisma** means that if Oprah endorses it, people love it.

One recent example: Since she became associated with Weight Watchers in 2015, membership has soared, including 600,000 new members just between 2017 and 2018.

In the years of her TV book club, an endorsement from her meant the book would sell an extra 600,000 to 800,000 copies.

Oprah gives millions of dollars to charities, and when she talks about one on TV, her fans donate, too.

OPRAH AS A SPIRITUAL LEADER

Although she is not a minister, some say a key to Oprah Winfrey's popularity is that she has the skills of a pastor. In 2001, she was chosen to lead the national prayer service in New York after the tragedy of 9/11. Why Oprah? She was the only American with the right combination of "spiritual leadership, celebrity recognition and consumer popularity" to lead the service, wrote religious studies scholar Kathryn Lofton.

Although raised as a Protestant Christian, today Oprah embraces a spirituality that draws from many religious traditions.

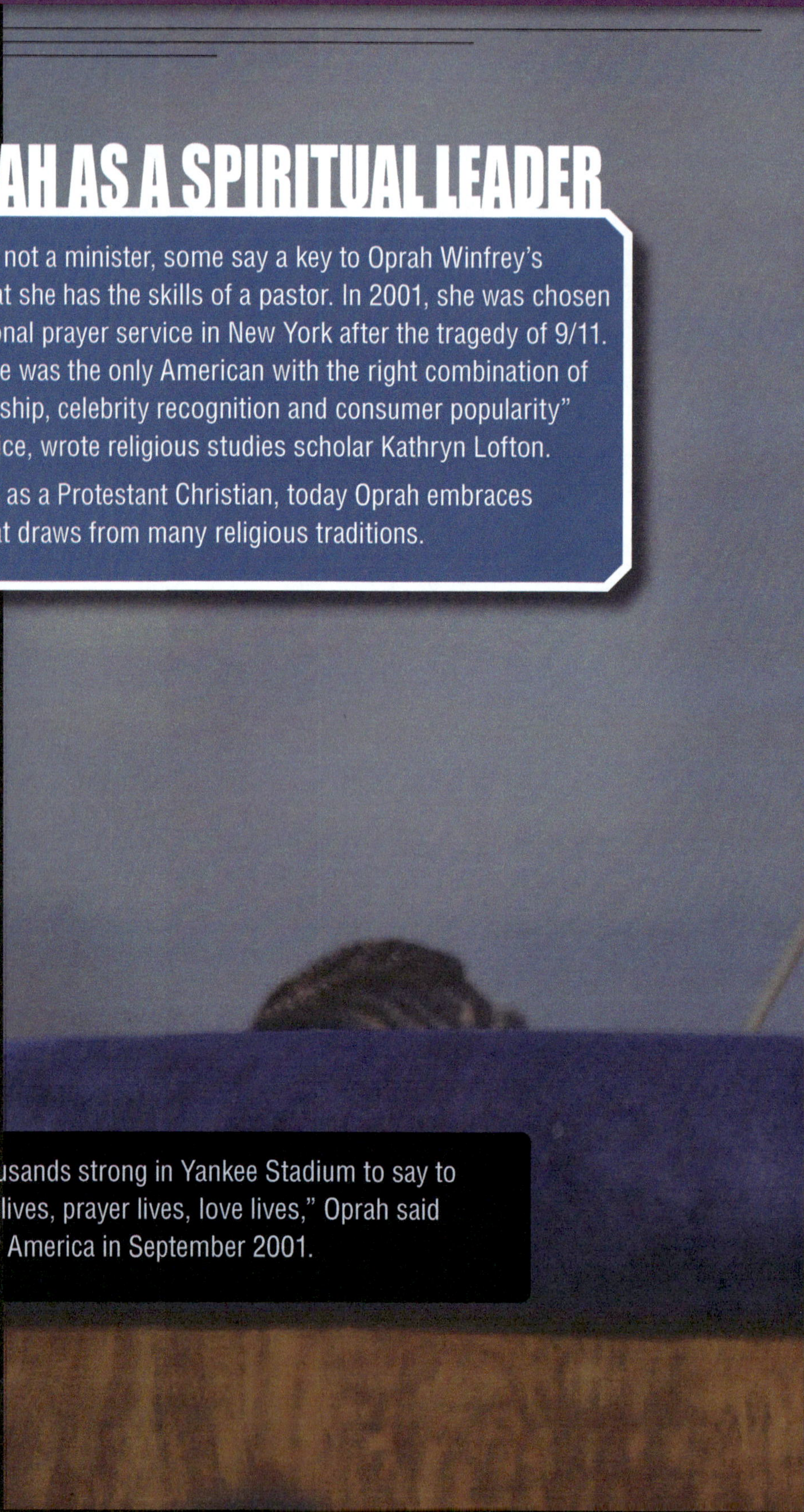

"We're here thousands strong in Yankee Stadium to say to the world: hope lives, prayer lives, love lives," Oprah said at the Prayer for America in September 2001.

Oprah used her massive influence to convince Congress to consider a proposal for a National Child Protection Act. Then, as a victim of childhood abuse, she testified about how the act was needed.

CHAPTER 5

ACTIVISM

Early in her career, Oprah was not a social activist. She never went on a protest march. She was too focused on climbing her way up the career ladder. Until 2000 she never had a politician on her show for fear of offending viewers. However, once she reached the pinnacle of her TV career, Oprah found she was powerful enough to create change. Two topics were important to her: education of girls and protection of girls from abuse. She also, for the first time, campaigned for a presidential candidate.

Here are four examples of her activism:

THE NATIONAL CHILD PROTECTION ACT

She testified before Congress in 1991 about the need for stronger laws to protect children from abuse through the National Child Protection Act, which would create a database to track child abusers. A version of the bill passed in 1993. Oprah was there when President Bill Clinton signed the new law. In 2008, her support also helped pass the PROTECT Our Children Act.

CAMPAIGNING FOR OBAMA

In 2008, Oprah came out strongly for Barack Obama, campaigned for him, and raised money to help get him elected president of the United States. Her strong endorsement, analysts said, helped turn out the vote so he won.

As early as 2006, Oprah was telling everyone that she hoped her favorite U.S. senator, Barack Obama of Illinois, would run for president. He was not well known nationally, but Oprah helped change that by campaigning for him. Crowds flocked to see Oprah and came away with admiration for the senator.

Oprah and the Obamas became good friends. After leaving office, Barack and Michelle vacationed on a cruise to Tahiti in 2017 with Oprah as one of their guests.

#METOO MOVEMENT

In 2017, many women in Hollywood came forward to say they had been sexually harassed by powerful men in the industry. Soon, people in many walks of life said, "me too," and the words became a Twitter hashtag. Oprah was one of the women to speak out. She recalled being harassed as a young reporter in the 1970s, but "I knew for sure that to report what was happening would have meant being labeled a problem — and the end of my career." She urged women to see that "our voices raised together can lead to systemic changes."

Oprah had the audience on their feet feet and applauding during her heartfelt speech at the Golden Globes in 2018.

HER INSPIRING SPEECH

In January 2018, Oprah Winfrey gave a grand speech on television accepting the Golden Globes Cecil B. DeMille Award for lifetime achievement. In it, she talked about the wave of women who stood up against sexual harassment in the #MeToo movement. She ended the speech with these words:

"In my career, what I've always tried my best to do, whether on television or through film, is to say something about how men and women really behave. To say how we experience shame, how we love and how we rage, how we fail, how we retreat, persevere and how we overcome. I've interviewed and portrayed people who've withstood some of the ugliest things life can throw at you, but the one quality all of them seem to share is an ability to maintain hope for a brighter morning, even during our darkest nights. So I want all the girls watching here, now, to know that a new day is on the horizon! And when that new day finally dawns, it will be because of a lot of magnificent women, many of whom are right here in this room tonight, and some pretty phenomenal men, fighting hard to make sure that they become the leaders who take us to the time when nobody ever has to say 'Me too' again."

Oprah is one of the most generous celebrities in the world. She says she takes charity personally by not thinking of money as "bits of paper and scraps of metal." Instead, as she wrote in *O Magazine*, she sees money as a bagful of flour, a can of soup. a blanket, or medicine for someone in need.

CHAPTER 6

OPRAH THE PHILANTHROPIST

As a billionaire, Oprah Winfrey lives the life of a very rich woman. Yet she has given away hundreds of millions of dollars to charity. She also has inspired others to become givers, multiplying her own gifts many times over. Her humanitarian work has inspired others.

OPRAH'S ANGEL NETWORK

In 1997, *The Oprah Winfrey Show* introduced Oprah's Angel Network. The first project was collecting pennies for charity. So many viewers participated that more than $3.5 million was raised for college scholarships for needy students. Angel Network challenged viewers to do something for charity — build a Habitat for Humanity home, collect pennies, or just help someone in need. By 2010 when it ended, viewers had raised $80 million for nearly 200 charitable projects around the world.

"WHEN YOU INVEST IN A YOUNG WOMAN YOU ARE INVESTING IN THE FUTURE, NOT ONLY OF SOUTH AFRICA BUT ALSO OF THE WORLD. SO THESE YOUNG LADIES ARE A SYMBOL AND A BEACON OF LIGHT, OF WHAT IS POSSIBLE."

– Message from Our Founder, Oprah Winfrey Leadership Academy for Girls website

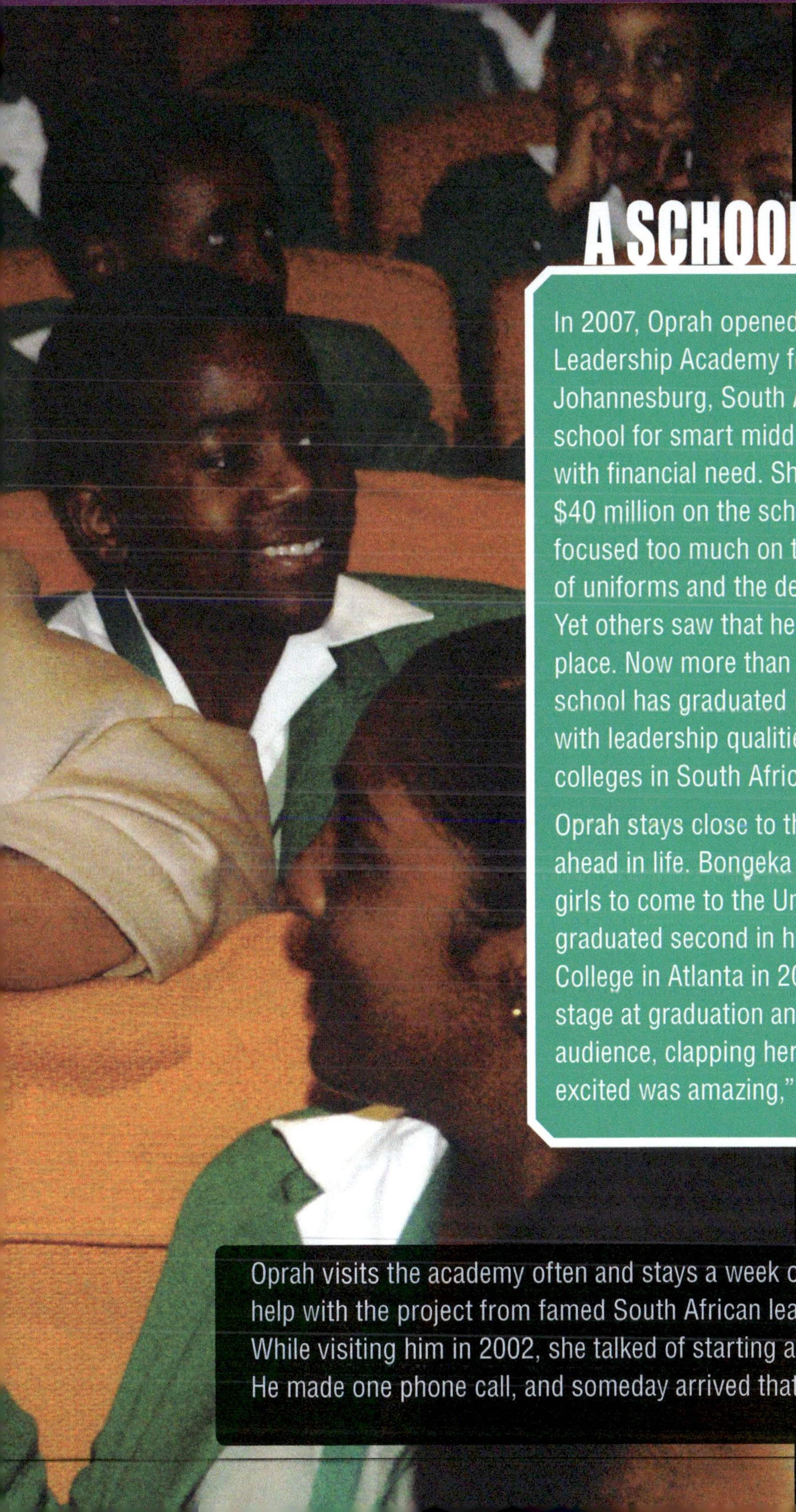

BUILDING A SCHOOL FOR GIRLS

In 2007, Oprah opened the Oprah Winfrey Leadership Academy for Girls near Johannesburg, South Africa. It is a boarding school for smart middle and high school girls with financial need. She spent an astonishing $40 million on the school, and critics said she focused too much on tiny things like the color of uniforms and the design of the pillowcases. Yet others saw that her heart was in the right place. Now more than 10 years along, the school has graduated many top students with leadership qualities who have gone on to colleges in South Africa and the United States.

Oprah stays close to the girls as they move ahead in life. Bongeka Zuma, one of the first girls to come to the United States for college, graduated second in her class at Spelman College in Atlanta in 2016. "Walking across the stage at graduation and seeing mom O in the audience, clapping her hands and just being so excited was amazing," she said.

Oprah visits the academy often and stays a week or more. She got special help with the project from famed South African leader Nelson Mandela. While visiting him in 2002, she talked of starting a school someday. He made one phone call, and someday arrived that very day!

President Barack Obama presented Oprah with the Presidential Medal of Freedom at the White House in 2013. She was honored for her work in broadcasting and her charitable giving and fund-raising. "Oprah's greatest strength has always been her ability to help us discover the best in ourselves," said the president.

OPRAH WINFREY CHARITABLE FOUNDATION

Begun in 2010, this foundation uses Oprah's own money to support charities worldwide. She **endowed** her foundation with about $240 million. Yet she has given away even more money than that.

EXAMPLES OF HER CHARITY

ACTIVISM

In 2018, she donated $500,000 to the March for Our Lives to support students marching for an end to gun violence.

MUSEUMS

She donated $12 million to the new Smithsonian National Museum of African American History and Culture in Washington, D.C. She also donated $1 million to the National Underground Railroad Freedom Center in Cincinnati.

SCHOOLS

She has given more than $400 million to educational causes, including 400 scholarships to Morehouse College, $10 million to A Better Chance program in Chicago that helped black students access better schools, nearly $1 million to her **alma mater** Tennessee State University for scholarships, and $40 million for the Oprah Winfrey Leadership Academy.

INTERNATIONAL

In 2002, she spent $7 million on Christmas Kindness, a program to give thousands of poor South African children gifts at Christmas.

EMERGENCY RELIEF

In 2005, she gave $10 million to help Hurricane Katrina victims.

GENEROSITY TO FAMILY

Generous to a fault, Oprah has given millions to her family and friends, plus paid for their cars, houses, vacations, school, weddings, and even drug rehab. Sometimes it is worthwhile, such as sending her nieces to college. Sometimes it doesn't work out well — in 2014 she had to get a court order to evict her father's ex-wife from a Nashville house Oprah had bought for the couple when they were married.

"TO MOVE FORWARD YOU HAVE TO GIVE BACK."

– Oprah Winfrey, commencement address at Stanford University, delivered June 15, 2008

In the 2018 movie *A Wrinkle in Time*, Oprah played Mrs. Which, one of the wisest and most powerful beings in the universe. Director Ava DuVernay thought that sounded like Oprah and invited her to do the film.

CHAPTER 7

THE FUTURE

Now in her 60s, Oprah Winfrey is still surprising America — and herself.

She recently became a part-time correspondent for the TV news program *60 Minutes*.

She still is the nation's only female African-American billionaire, worth nearly $3 billion. She is still a producer, actress, and businesswoman.

She writes peaceful, uplifting columns for *O Magazine* and interviews spiritual writers and thinkers on her *Super Soul Sunday* podcast. She feels at home in both California and Hawaii, surrounded by her friends, dogs, nature, and peace.

> "SPEAKING YOUR TRUTH IS THE MOST POWERFUL TOOL WE ALL HAVE."
>
> *– Oprah Winfrey's Cecil B. DeMille award speech, January 2018*

Yet, she still can give a barn burner of a speech. She was widely praised for her 2018 Golden Globes speech about the power of women. Afterward, one headline proclaimed she was still "the most charismatic person in America."

She has "the kind of cultural **cachet** usually reserved for saintly figures like Mr. Rogers or the Pope," wrote *Newsweek* magazine.

In 2018, some people began encouraging her to run for president of the United States. She said she was not interested, but she did not definitely turn down the idea.

Oprah Winfrey has never been a shrinking violet, and she likely will not start now. As a woman who won't be silenced, she continues to speak out and take action on behalf of women and girls.

What's next for her? As they say on television, stay tuned.

"THE BIGGEST ADVENTURE YOU CAN EVER TAKE IS TO LIVE THE LIFE OF YOUR DREAMS."

– www.oprah.com

OPRAH'S LOVE OF DOGS

She has loved dogs since she was a child. At one point as an adult she had 11 dogs! As of 2018, Oprah reportedly had five dogs: golden retrievers Luke and Layla, cocker spaniel Sadie, and springer spaniels Lauren and Sunny. Sadie, Lauren, and Sunny were all adopted from PAWS Chicago, a no-kill animal shelter.

Her favorite dog was her cocker spaniel, Sophie, who died in 2008 at age 13.

"Over the years I have felt the truest, purest love — the love of God, really, I imagine that's what God's love feels like — is the love that comes from your dog," Oprah said in 2014.

Oprah took her chocolate-brown cocker spaniel Solomon everywhere and he became quite a celebrity, too. Solomon (1994-2008) was a gift from her life partner Stedman Graham.

> "YOU ARE BUILT NOT TO SHRINK DOWN TO LESS BUT TO BLOSSOM INTO MORE."
>
> *– Oprah Winfrey's book* What I Know for Sure, *page 109*

Oprah is not short at 5 foot 7 inches, but Stedman makes her look that way! The former college basketball player is about a foot taller.

OPRAH'S PARTNER STEDMAN GRAHAM

The quiet partner of Oprah Winfrey for more than 30 years has been Stedman Graham. They met at a charity event in Chicago and began dating in 1986. After getting engaged in 1992, they decided not to marry. Instead, they have a "spiritual union" as life partners. "I just support her in her life. And she supports me in my life," Stedman says. As Oprah's biggest booster, he has been encouraging her to run for president for decades and even offering to work on her campaign.

Stedman's own life couldn't be more full. The New Jersey native has an educational, marketing, and management company, and he is a multimillionaire in his own right. He has written 11 self-help and motivational books, including two best sellers. He founded a charity to help teens. He has a daughter, Wendy, from a past marriage. Oprah and Stedman are doting grandparents to Wendy's daughter Cadence, born in 2015.

When Oprah accepted a lifetime achievement award at the Golden Globes awards program in 2018, she called Stedman "my rock."

RECOGNITION

FILM, TELEVISION, AND AWARDS

FILM

She has acted in *The Color Purple* in 1985, *Native Son* in 1986, *Beloved* in 1998, *Lee Daniels' The Butler* in 2013, *Selma* in 2014, and *A Wrinkle in Time* in 2018; she also did voices for several animated films such as *Charlotte's Web* in 2006.

TELEVISION

She was a newscaster in Nashville and Baltimore from 1973 to 1976; co-host of *People Are Talking* from 1977 to 1984 in Baltimore; then host of *AM Chicago* (later called *The Oprah Winfrey Show*) from 1984 to 2011, the highest-rated talk show of all time. Since then she has hosted shows on the OWN cable network and been a special correspondent for CBS *60 Minutes* since 2017. She also has guest-starred on many TV shows and TV movies, such as *The Immortal Life of Henrietta Lacks* in 2017.

PRODUCER

In addition to *The Oprah Winfrey Show* and shows on the OWN network, she has produced many films, TV shows, and *The Color Purple* on Broadway.

A FEW AWARDS SHE'S WON

A full list of Oprah Winfrey's honors would go on for pages, but here are some of the most notable:

16 Daytime Emmy Awards for *The Oprah Winfrey Show* as outstanding host and outstanding talk show

Academy Award nomination as best supporting actress for *The Color Purple*, 1985

Inducted into the National Women's Hall of Fame, Seneca Falls, New York, 1994

One of the 50 Most Beautiful People in the World, 1997, *People Magazine*

Bob Hope Humanitarian Award at the 2002 Emmy Awards

Academy Award winner for humanitarian endeavors (Jean Hersholt Humanitarian Award), 2011

Kennedy Center honoree, 2010

Presidential Medal of Freedom, 2013

Golden Globes Cecil B. DeMille Award for lifetime achievement, 2018

TIMELINE

1954
Born January 29, 1954, in Kosciusko, Mississippi to Vernita Lee and Vernon Winfrey

1971-75
Attends Tennessee State University, majoring in speech and drama

1973
Gets job as newscaster at WTVF-TV Channel 5 Nashville

1976
Lands job as news anchor at WJZ-TV in Baltimore, Maryland

1984
Hired to host *AM Chicago* on WLS-TV

1985
Stars as Sofia in the movie *The Color Purple*

1991
Advocates for National Child Protection Act to protect children from child abusers

1996
Starts Oprah's book club on her show

1997
Starts Oprah's Angel Network, a foundation for charity

2000
Launches *O Magazine*

2006
Launches Oprah & Friends channel on satellite radio

2007
Opens a school in South Africa

2010
Kennedy Center awards honoree

2011
Last episode of *The Oprah Winfrey Show* runs September 9. Creates Oprah Winfrey cable network (OWN).

2013
Awarded Presidential Medal of Freedom

2016
Wins Tony Award as a co-producer for revival of *The Color Purple* on Broadway

2017
Becomes special correspondent for CBS's *60 Minutes*

2018
Gets Cecil B. DeMille Award for lifetime achievement at Golden Globes

GLOSSARY

alma mater: The school or college that a person attended.

cachet: A special quality that makes a person admired or respected; prestige.

charisma: A magnetic personality that draws others to you.

empathy: A quality of being able to know how another person feels.

endowed: Put a sum of money in a bank account or investment to be used for a foundation's charity work.

icon: An individual who is highly successful and greatly admired.

lurid: Overly shocking or sensational.

mediocre: Moderate or low quality.

philanthropist: A person who gives away money for good causes.

skinheads: People who shave their heads, usually young white people who have racist ideas and may belong to a gang.

syndicated: When a TV show is sold for use on many stations, not just one.

FOR MORE INFORMATION

BOOKS

Dakers, Diane. *Oprah Winfrey: Media Legend and Inspiration to Millions*. New York, NY: Crabtree Publishing Company, 2016.

Jones, Jen. *Oprah Winfrey: Celebrity with Heart.* Berkeley Heights, NJ: Enslow Publishers, 2011.

Lies, Anne. *Oprah Winfrey: Media Mogul.* Edina, MN: ABDO Publishing Company, 2011.

WEBSITES

www.Oprah.com
Oprah Winfrey's website

www.supersoul.tv
Super Soul Sunday website

INDEX